Talk With Love

SPIRE BOOKS

Fleming H. Revell Company   Old Tappan, New Jersey

by permission
Bible Voice, Inc.
Van Nuys, California

CONTENTS

TO

My parents, Harold and Francis
My wife and closest friend, Donna
Our children, Shawna Dee and Shane

PROLOGUE

It may come as a surprise to many, whether you are a practicing Christian, a Jew, an agnostic or an athiest your marriage is based on traditions that date back hundreds of years to Judeo-Christian Holy writings. With or without your awareness these traditions have a strong influence on your most personal, most intimate relationship.

Most traditions arise from practices that originally were both meaningful and practical. A custom may continue as tradition, even though it is no longer of practical value and the circumstances that made it meaningful no longer exist. Traditions are perpetuated to provide a link with our past. Some traditions may be perpetuated even though they are downright burdensome in the present.

There can be no doubt that the traditional marriage is in trouble. Is it simply a tradition we carry on for tradition's sake, trying to conform to its roles without even knowing why we try? Is it an institution bereft of present prupose, the benefit of which has been long lost, a tradition carried as a dead weight long past burial time?

That which is traditional may seem to have no contemporary value, not because its original objective is without value in today's market place, but because it has become detached from its original purpose and is carried on as an empty symbol; that is, it represents but no longer contains the principles that once gave it a place of honor and respect.

This book is the result of an examination of Hebrew and Christian Scriptures in search of such principles, non-optional principles that might be recaptured and re-incorporated into the marriage relationship to make it as significant to human need today as at any time in the past.

Doug Roberts, M.D.

Chapter 1

THE DREAM

Do you remember the dream you had in your heart as you stood that day in the presence of those witnesses? It was a good dream. You came into this world because at some time a man and a woman got together. Since your arrival, social, psychological and later physiological pressures were urging, not forcing, but urging you toward marriage.

Where would marriage take you? The answer was in the dream. There may have been an element of unreality in your youthful understanding of that dream but God had put it there.

JOSEPH

God put a dream in the heart of a youth named Joseph. It took thirteen years of patience and hard work, years marked with periods of stress and despair, to change that pampered teenager into a man capable of fulfilling the dream as prime minister under Pharoah, King of Egypt.

God has a goal or purpose for our lives, the full extent of which reaches beyond our range of vision. Often all we have is a dream. It would have been a bit too heavy if God had clued Joseph in on all that lay ahead of him. God had as a goal a hiding place where He could preserve the germ of a nation. He put a dream in Joseph's heart to get him started.

Joseph saw himself in a high position. We always see ourselves close to the top in our dreams, otherwise we refer to them as nightmares. We see ourselves as successful, acclaimed, our company and our services in demand. These dreams, especially day-dreams, provide some of the stimulus that keeps us going.

God was concerned with more than Joseph's status. He was planning to use that status to a more valuable end. Status, prominence, prestige can be used to good advantage. Some of us are so dedicated to poverty and obscurity we would not allow God to advance us.

GOAL AND PURPOSE

God wants your dream to come true. He has also a goal for your marriage, a purpose

8

of providing service; to serve the needs of another human being, to care for children and nurture them to adulthood.

Your dream fulfillment, your own happiness in marriage is linked to that purpose. If you will not fulfill that purpose in marriage your personal happiness and fulfillment in marriage will be frustrated.

Thousands of people pursuing pleasure may never find the object of their search. Pleasure does not exist by itself. It is found only in combination with fulfilled purpose. Pleasure is not an end product. It is a by-product.

THE HAZARDS

Several years ago I set out to climb Mount Kilimanjaro, the highest mountain in Africa. It has two peaks. The highest rises to 19,200 feet. The party was comprised of British, American and Canadian diplomatic officials plus members of the Tanzanian and Canadian Armed Forces. I was a member of the latter group. During the ascent, we rested one night at a camp situated at 15,000 feet. Emmanuel, our guide, woke us at one a.m. to begin the last 4,000 feet of our climb. The most difficult part of the climb was to tolerate the altitude. He said we were starting early so we would be able to view the sunrise from the summit. We arrived at daybreak.

Then he told us the truth. Most of us

were inexperienced at mountain climbing. Had we started in daylight and been able to see the climb ahead of us, we would have given up before we started. Having only his light and voice to guide us, we accomplished, one step at a time, a task we would otherwise have never attempted.

You started off your marriage without any experience in matrimony. Had you been aware of the shallows, the rip-tides and the dangerous shoals your ship would have to navigate, or the storms that would beset it, you may never have embarked on the voyage.

Maybe it was fortunate you were aware only of the excitement that the presence of your beloved created in you. Had someone counselled you to prepare for a few squalls, you might have heard his words. His counsel may apply to ordinary marriages but certainly not to *yours*. The mystic ecstasy of love would carry you and *your* mate over the turmoils that others have to go through.

UNCERTAINTY

At least that may be how you felt if you were married fifteen or twenty years ago. Today, people may not feel that sort of unquestioned confidence. Young people have seen so many marriages fail they are not at all sure they can trust in such self-confidence. Patients tell me they don't know one happily married couple. Children, hearing of the divorce of relatives and neighbors fear for the future of their own home and parents.

Young adults become extremely susceptible to suggestions being made by people experiencing the same fears: —

"Have a trial marriage before you really commit yourself."

"Experiment before marriage to be sure you are compatible."

"Don't get tied up with a paper contract. Marriage is for happiness. If you aren't happy with the first partnership, get out of it and get lined-up with someone else."

"It is hard to get out of a legal marriage. Live common law. It is much easier to get out of it then. You just say good-bye and split."

"You have to consider yourself first. Don't let social pressures, or promises you made before you knew what you were getting into, or the fact you have children, hold you to the ball and chain. If your marriage has become a drag, move on. It is better for the children anyway."

THAT PIECE OF PAPER

I am personally grateful for the paper contract and the memory of pledges Donna and I have made to each other. If our frail bark had not been undergirded by these and by the influence of society, church and family, we would have beached our boat, left it awash and gone our separate ways.

The glue of two lovely children, who deserved a stable home in a world they never asked to enter, helped us from becoming unstuck.

We had made a commitment to each other. We believed in the permanency of marriage. This held us together long enough to learn something of the principles involved — some of the rules of the road, so we could build a marriage, the building of which is an exciting adventure and a satisfying experience.

If you enter marriage with a plan of escape filed in your mind, believe me, you will find adequate reasons to use it.

I place great value on the marriage contract. It contains three essential ingredients required for a successful marriage and assumes a fourth.

Acceptance
The first ingredient is the total acceptance of each other. I, Doug, do take thee, Donna to be my lawfully wedded wife . . . for richer, for poorer, for better, for worse, in sickness and in health . . .

Commitment
A second ingredient is commitment. A pledge is made to live together . . . to love,

to honor . . . and *forsaking* all others *keep myself* only unto you.

Permanence
The third ingredient is permanence . . . to have and to hold from this day forward until death us do part.

Maturity
The assumed ingredient is maturity. We assume that the participants speaking the marriage vows have the maturity required to fulfill them.

THE ESCAPE

For many of us little conscious thought is given to marriage until it is in trouble. You were young and single. Life was a hassle. There were problems at home; problems with father and mother; problems between father and mother; problems with brothers and sisters. You felt lonely and unfulfilled. It seemed no one understood you until your sweetheart came along.

Loneliness, misunderstanding, frustration, emptiness, the blues, problems, problems, and more problems — marriage would solve all that.

Even the courtship had its ups and downs. You thought it was because social attitudes prevented you from fully expressing those powerful feelings you had for each other. Marriage would solve that problem.

Some people get married to escape problems. Marriage doesn't eliminate problems. It creates a set of its own.

The dream is still there. At least it was yesterday, but how do you make it work?

Now you are thinking, "Maybe it was all wrong. Maybe we started on the wrong basis. We were physically attracted to each other. Marriage is spiritual and other things and we didn't have any of that when we started. Other people knew it wouldn't work and they warned me. Maybe they were right. Maybe I married the wrong person."

Chapter 2

BACHELOR MARRIAGE COUNSELLOR

"The Pharisees also came unto him, tempting him, and saying unto him, Is it lawful for a man to put away his wife for every cause? And he answered and said unto them. Have ye not read, that he which made them at the beginning made them male and female, And said, For this cause shall a man leave father and mother, and shall cleave to his wife: and they twain shall be one flesh? Wherefore they are no more twain, but one flesh. What therefore God hath joined together, let not man put asunder.

"They say unto him, Why did Moses then command to give a writing of divorcement, and to put her away? He saith unto them. Moses because of the hardness of your hearts suffered you to put away your wives: but from the beginning it was not so. And I say unto you, Whosoever shall put away his wife, except it be for fornication, and shall marry another, committeth adultery: and whoso marrieth her which is put away doth commit adultery" (Matthew 19:3-8).

This group of married men came to a bachelor for marriage counselling.

"Is it right for a man to put away his wife for any reason?" That is the question of a man who has made up his mind what he wants to do. He just hopes he can make it look good. With a little push most anything will pass for incompatability or mental cruelty. His wife has burned the toast for the third consecutive morning.

In our time wives have also the right to initiate divorce proceedings.

I hear wives and husbands accuse each other: —

> "He doesn't love me any more."
>
> "We are not happy together."
>
> "My husband doesn't share my faith. How can we be one? How can he give spiritual leadership to the home?"
>
> "My wife won't have any part with the charismatic renewal."
>
> "We don't have anything in common."
>
> "I'm not happy."
>
> "My husband isn't the man he was when I married him."

16

"We don't agree on how to raise the children."

"I don't get anything out of sex with my wife."

These and dozens of other statements can be paraded into court as incompatability or mental cruelty.

Many marriages have problems, serious problems. They look hopeless. There are marriages in which people are doing terrible things to each other.

These men came to get an opinion on the morality of divorce. As you read between the lines of the above scripture, you get the impression Jesus put his finger on a different spot.

Moses knew how desperately cruel a man could be to his wife. He may also have known something of what it is like to face a woman whose tongue is armed with razor blades.

THE LEGALIST

There are two extreme positions on the subject of divorce. The seemingly cold, hard-nosed legalist says divorce is an absolute wrong. You are in it and you have to stay in it. Draw the blinds so the neighbors won't find out your fight. Try to keep the blood off the walls. Above everything else don't mar the reputation of the church by getting a divorce or letting out the secret that even Christians have problems. This counsel is often given with the understanding that if it is not heeded, the divorcee, especially if remarried, will find his or her status permanently altered.

THE LIBERAL

The advice from the opposite camp is that marriage is just a paper contract. If it is not working, tear up the paper and start over again with someone else.

No one has ever come to me saying, "My piece of paper is tearing. Please glue it together again." There is more than paper being torn. Willingly or unwillingly, intentionally or unintentionally, a man and a woman who enter the intimate relationship of marriage, experience a union beyond paper glue. That union cannot be disrupted without hurt and loss.

I believe Jesus was in neither camp. He upheld the desirability of a permanent marriage, but made people recognize the real problem — their treatment of each other, their hardness of heart.

God is not so much against divorce as He is against the hardness of heart — the cruelty with which two people treat each other that divorce is inevitable.

It is not a matter of marrying the right person. It is a matter of right treatment to the person you married.

God is against divorce, not because it mars the reputation of the Christian church

18

but because of the wounds caused to the man and the woman — wounds that are often contaminated with resentment, bitterness and self-pity and carried un-healed into a second marriage.

I am against divorce because of the guilt and pain it brings to children — adding to the insecurity of months or years of domestic civil war.

People who have experienced divorce are well aware of the pain. You can't put your heart into a marriage, then have it torn apart, without suffering loss.

A BETTER WAY

Perhaps one of the most insincere state-ments made by people about the Lord is, "I believe Jesus was a great teacher." If a significant part or the whole of my life was messed up and I thought someone was a great teacher, I would crack open his Book and see what He had to say. If you are looking for life, for purpose in life or meaningful alteration to your life, I recom-mend you start reading The Book. I sup-pose there is a mystical character to God that I know nothing about, but I know Him in a practical manner that relates to the need and purpose of my life.

In His answer to the Pharisees, Jesus did not limit His involvement to a public stand against divorce.

He made reference to the beginning. He

recalled a blue-print for marriage that required the development of an emotional, physical, intellectual, spiritual, social, cultural union: a union that leaves each individual intact but united with the other.

Does that sound a bit heavy? Someone reads this and says, "I'd be satisfied if I could just get along with my husband."

Don't interpret Christ's remarks as reference to a super human ideal that can only make marriage more burdensome. Aspiring to goals that are beyond us leaves us with a feeling of failure and depression. He spoke of the purpose of God not with the intent of crushing you under its responsibility but with the intent of seeing it fulfilled in your life. He came to reveal the will of the Father — not revelation by intellectual discovery alone, but revelation through personal experience. He is not satisfied to have you know His will, He will enable you to experience it in your own life.

Much of the inspiration in this book comes from the experience in my own marriage. This is not designed to project our marriage as some flawless example. I suppose our marriage could be perfect except for two reasons. I am one of them.

Christ did not come to increase the burden of marriage with further idealism. He came to make it workable by changing the people involved.

Up to now you have probably been trying to change your mate. You have no authority to do that. You are responsible only for yourself. You may not be responsible for becoming the way you are. The things you have gone through have possibly made you that way. Perhaps you are not responsible for having become as you are, *but you are responsible for staying that way.* Maybe you can justify the fact that you have become resentful, irritable, unloving, unresponsive, hurt or bitter, but you cannot justify remaining that way.

What is more, you stand a mighty good chance of carrying those same problems into your next marriage, so you may as well work them out in this one.

HOW DO I CHANGE?

How do I change? That is where the Good News comes in. I am not ashamed of the Good News because it is the power of God to change every person who believes it. There is power available through the Holy Spirit to make you the kind of wife you dreamed of being — to make you the kind of man, husband and father you always wanted to be.

I am persuaded that every person you will ever meet has a greater desire for honor, a greater love of decency and dignity than he would dare let anyone know. Most of you would be amazed to learn how much your spouse desires to please you, to make you happy — but doesn't know how — thinks you don't care and has given up.

Marriages fail not when they go to the divorce courts, but when they stop progressing toward the goal — when the couple stops trying.

If we wish to stem the rising tide of divorce, halt the epidemic of broken homes, it is not enough to increase resistance to divorce. It is important we underscore the permanency of the marriage relationship, but we must offer something constructive to troubled marriages, pour oil and wine into wounded men and women, minister grace and counsel to people who have become bruised and bound — who feel trapped in a seemingly endless merry-go-round of attack and counter-attack.

MERCY AND TRUTH ARE COME TOGETHER

God is against divorce, but He is not against divorcees nor against candidates for divorce.

Jesus was not embarrassed to identify himself with people in trouble. He was the champion of social outcasts. Since His resurrection He has continued to champion the cause of people who are in trouble.

He is not satisfied simply to have you continue in marriage, He wants you to develop in marriage.

Secret strife and disguised resentment are as far from the mark as divorce.

We may be tempted to hide the embarrassment and pain of marital strife, to encourage the masquerade, to suffer in silence. We may be tempted to quit trying, divide the goods and the children and go our separate ways. The pain in the children's eyes as they witness the turmoil may convince you there would be less harm in a divorce than in continuing the present existence. There are moments when you are really happy together, but you don't seem to know how to stop hurting each other. You don't like what it is doing to either of you. Surely, you think, divorce would be better than this.

There is a third alternative. Neither divorce nor continuing strife but a harmonious union — a union that will require faith, love, courage, patience, intelligence and common sense.

If, however, you have followed the second route: if you have gone through the tragic causes and fact of a divorce and have now found a meaningful and happy marriage, I thank God with you. God's blessing is as available to you as to any other person under heaven.

Chapter 3
THE GIFT

It is interesting to examine the Judeo-Christian explanation of the origin of marriage. We can find it at the front of The Book, in Genesis Chapter Two. Marriage had its beginning in the Book of beginnings.

This Book used to give me a lot of trouble. As a child I had been taught to believe it to be true. As a student, it seemed so far removed from what I was learning at the University that it seemed irrelevant. It doesn't trouble me anymore. The better I know the Lord the easier it is to believe the things He says.

God said it was not good for man to be alone. He said "I will make for him a helper appropriate to his needs."

I recall a lunch I had with several of my colleagues. One of us, a consultant in psychiatry, asked if he could pray before we ate. He offered thanks with the following prayer.

"Father, I thank you that you love us and that you show your love in appropriate ways by meeting our needs."

God loved Adam. A gift was sought that would express God's love and meet Adam's need.

In all His creation there was nothing found to be adequate, so God designed one to meet the specifications.

WOUNDS

Adam was given a general anaesthetic. His chest was opened, a rib removed and the incision closed. The wound healed.

Marriages don't happen painlessly. Paul wasn't just whistling through his teeth when he said those that marry shall have trouble. Married people do hurt each other.

Marriages aren't made in heaven or in the church. Marriages are made in the home as two people, differing in many ways, work to overcome the obstacles in their path. The reward is well worth the effort.

The effort is a challenge. The achievement doesn't come through thinking happy thoughts or waving a magic wand. It is hammered out. In a workshop of pain and problems, discouragement and disagreement, tears and trials, your dream is reshaped by the hammer of time on the anvil of reality.

Even unintentional wounds hurt. Medicated with love and forgiveness the wounds will heal without the contamination of resentment and without deforming, disfiguring scars.

THE GIFT

From the rib, God fashioned His love-gift, wrapped it in a beautiful package — a package so beautiful that men have trouble keeping their hands off — and He inscribed a little card,

TO: Adam,
With Love
From God

Adam woke up in the recovery room. There she stood in all her splendor. Wow! What a convalescence.

She returned during visiting hours carrying an apple.

THE BAD WITH THE GOOD

Marriage isn't made of all plus factors. There are some negatives. These must be accommodated. Each of us comes to marriage bringing some good and some not so good qualities.

Throughout our childhood we develop behavior patterns. Most of them are absorbed unconsciously. Marriage behavior is included in these patterns. We arrive in marriage, consciously or unconsciously "knowing" how a man treats a woman, what a man's and a woman's role is in marriage, what is expected of each other. You had a clear picture of how your husband should treat you. Unfortunately, he had learned in a somewhat different school and had a slightly different idea of how a wife should be treated. You "knew" exactly what was expected of a wife. His expectations were a bit different. He "knew" what was expected of a husband. You had a different set of expectations.

Perhaps worse, you entered marriage not having any idea of what to bring with you. You thought you were supposed to know and you couldn't let on to anyone you didn't know. So now you are trying to bluff your way through.

There is, in each of us, some things our mates admire and some things that bug them. Some of these bugs may never be worked out of us. We have to make adjustments to each other. Good apples, rotten apples, no apples at all, we come to marriage as we are and we totally accept each other with a largeness of heart that allows mutual development and forbids stifling.

POLYGAMY — MONOGOMY

God made a woman for Adam. He made *one* woman.

There are those who say that men by nature are polygamists. That reminds me of the man who traded his forty-year old wife for two twenties and then found out he wasn't wired for two twenty.

Whatever a man's abilities or inclinations might be, polygomy may elevate his status and enhance his ego. If his many wives are all out working and turning their wages over to him he may even be more prosperous. Polygamy, however, does nothing for the status of the woman.

It may be that in many societies, faced with the choice, a woman would prefer to be number three or number five wife rather than to be no wife at all. Women in a society oriented to monogomy would probably choose to be unmarried. A position in a harem, even as number one wife is too far below the status they have learned to expect for a married woman.

Contrary to what many of its vocal critics have to say, the Christian concept of marriage enhances the status of women. The problem is that men are often the poorest practitioners of their faith when they are at home.

Eve was God's gift to Adam. Did you ever stop to think that the person who has been putting up with you all these years is God's love gift to you?

Women have a right to hold their heads high. They are a special creation.

That special creation was made a gift to

men. Men also have a right to hold their heads high but with humility. That gift should be received with appreciation and treated in a manner relative to the prestige of the Giver. It is possible that a man will answer to God for the treatment he gives his wife. Perhaps someone should sound a warning. Perhaps wives should come with a warning label affixed:

HANDLE WITH CARE
or
ANSWER TO THE MANUFACTURER

God said He would make for Adam a helper appropriate to his needs. In His wisdom He made a woman.

I wonder if God would allow us to question His wisdom. He seems to be terribly confident in Himself. He probably wouldn't feel threatened by our queries.

Someone has said, God made man and rested. God made woman and neither God nor man has rested since.

Sometimes I ask couples, and I especially like to ask the husband, "Why did God make a woman to meet Adam's needs? Why didn't he make another man?"

A man is pretty physical in his understanding of need. The husband fidgets. He's onto sex already. I can see the wheels turning in his head. He turns in his chair and checks to see if the door from the consulting room is open. He might have to get out in a hurry. This doctor must be a bit strange. Imagine asking a question like that.

Yes, he is thinking about sex alright, but he is not going to admit it. He is going to say something more sophisticated.

He mumbles, "Well, hu .. uh .. God made a woman for ... well ... uh ... re-creation. . recreation ... no, no, that's not the word ... procreation; that's the word I want.

"Is that why you have sexual intercourse?. . . for procreation, I mean?" No answer. His wife giggles.

Adam may not have had a sex drive ... until he saw Eve. She may have had as much to do with stimulating it as she had to do with relieving it. Just think of the problems that would be eliminated if women kept themselves out of sight.

That procreation idea is a pretty fair answer except for one thing. You are dealing with a genius. God didn't have to make use of sexual reproduction. He could have figured out some other method. I'm glad He didn't.

Eve's arrival paved the way for a future generation. She arrived, however, for Adam's benefit. There were purposes to be served in addition to procreation. The patient wasn't so wrong as he thought. The word recreation may not be so far off the mark.

31

SEX IS FUN

The sexual relationship meets the need or desire for procreation and it meets physical need. The normal sexual relationship also lends itself to meeting psychological needs that are just as basic to the marriage relationship and maybe more important than the physical component.

A normal sexual relationship is a relationship between two mutually consenting, mature adults of the opposite sex who have linked themselves together in a permanent relationship condusive to establishing a home and rearing children. Please do not take this to mean that a childless relationship or a relationship in which conception is thwarted is abnormal.

Most couples want children. Infertility is a disappointment to them. The sexual relationship, however, has meaning and purpose apart from reproduction and continues to be meaningful and purposeful after the family circle has been filled.

If I were not a Christian I could possibly support the traditional attitude of many church people toward sex: the attitude that sex is unclean, a subject of embarrassment, enshrouded in guilt, a bit shameful — certainly not to be enjoyed.

God takes the credit for creating sex. Male and female, He created them. That is sex. God looked at what He had made and said it was good. With a clear conscience, every husband and wife can say, "Amen, Father what you have made is very good."

In many Bibles, the footnotes to the Songs of Solomon state that this portion of the Bible illustrates the love that Jesus Christ has for His Church. If that is so, it is a most powerful, scriptural validation and approval of the relationship between a man and his wife. The Songs of Solomon describe the delight they find in each other's body and the joys of the bed chamber.

(The Songs of Solomon are in the Old Testament, if you are looking for them.)

INSTITUTED TO SERVE

The point to be underscored is that marriage was designed to meet needs. We would be terribly hard-bitten if we were to assume that the woman was created to meet the needs of the man, period. The woman also has needs. In both the Old[1] and the New[2] Testaments the woman's needs are recognized and the man's responsibility to meet those needs is clearly stated.

We all come to marriage with needs we want met. We come to marriage without experience. We each have to learn how to meet the needs of the other.

---

1. Exodus 21:4-11; Exodus 22:16; Deuteronomy 21:11-17; Deuteronomy 22:11-18; Deuteronomy 24:1-15; Malachi 2:13-16.
2. Matthew 19:5; Mark 10:7; I Corinthians 7:33; Ephesians 5:25, 28, 29; I Timothy 5:8; I Peter 3:7.

A successful marriage is the result of us lovingly meeting each other's needs. We direct our attention to the needs of our partner, rather than to our own. We must exercise patience with respect to our own needs, allowing our partner to learn how to please us.

The pleasure of marriage is as much obtained from meeting our partner's need as it is from having our own needs met.

If our needs are not met eventually, we become dissatisfied and resentful. Too often people enter marriage terribly immature, terribly occupied with their own needs, terribly intolerant of any delay in the gratification of their needs.

Chapter 4

YOU ARE THE GREATEST

Cruising in the Caribbean I laid in my bunk thinking about our home. I started to read Ephesians. I sat up in amazement when I finished reading the fifth chapter. I saw something that turned the light on in my brain. The husband is three times instructed to love his wife, yet the wife is not once instructed to love her husband.

"Husbands, love your wives, even as Christ also loved the church, and gave himself for it."

"So ought men to love their wives as their own bodies. He that loveth his wife loveth himself."

"Nevertheless, let everyone of you in particular so love his wife even as himself."

It seems a man who doesn't love himself would be a poor candidate for matrimony.

LOVE IS THE GREATEST

This repetition of instruction suggests that the woman's most crucial need is to be loved. Certainly, most every woman who has ever talked to me about her unhappy marriage has had the lack of love from her husband as her chief complaint.

"My husband doesn't love me anymore."

"My husband never tells me that he loves me."

"There is no love left in our marriage."

"He doesn't love me. All he wants is sex. He just loves himself."

This tells me what *she* feels is most lacking in her marriage.

There were no instructions given to the wives to love their husbands. Does this mean the husbands do not want or need to be loved? No, it means that there is another word that better describes man's most critical need — what he most wants from his wife.

LOVE IS LEARNED

So far as the love is concerned, Paul did give instructions elsewhere[1] that the mature women were to teach the young women to love their husbands. Now that sort of stops you short, doesn't it? We always thought to love was to do what

---

1. Titus 2:3,4

comes naturally. Here we find out it is something we have to be taught. To love is something we have to learn. Back to school we go.

No doubt about it, husbands want to be loved. They may let on they don't. They are big and tough and don't need any of that mushy stuff. A clever woman will quickly see through that front and fill the need without letting on that she saw it.

Men want to be loved, but what they most need from their wives is best described by another word. That word is *admiration*.

YOU'RE THE GREATEST

Let the wife see that she deeply respects and reverences her husband, and she honors him, prefers him, esteems him, praises him and admires him exceedingly.

I expect there is no creature under heaven more proud than the human male. I'm not speaking of conceit, arrogance or haughtiness. I am speaking of an inspired inner drive, a drive which is a combination of dignity, self-esteem and self-assurance, the desire to, and the confidence in, his ability to achieve.

It gives him the courage to try and having failed, to try again. It involves his manhood, his masculinity. It provides him with a certain aggressiveness and energizes him to leadership. Every man is required to assume leadership at some level and to some degree.

Undisciplined, this drive could turn him into a power-hungry tyrant: destroyed, it leaves his insides shrivelled-up like a dried prune.

I suspect this drive is inherent — inborn. It may be culturally induced through a learned masculine role. I doubt this. I believe it was instilled in creation. God told Adam and Eve to have dominion over every living thing. It takes a powerful internal drive to rise to a position of authority or dominion.

Whatever the source of this drive in a man, it is not self-sustaining nor of independent origin. It requires input from others. He must be esteemed by someone besides himself. His greatest benefit is from the esteem of the person most intimately acquainted with him — his wife.

What he wants most from the marriage is the admiration of his wife, the assurance that she is one hundred percent behind him. Knowing his faults better than anyone else and more aware than any, of his weaknesses, she still stands by him, and expresses confidence in him.

A man wants his wife to brag about him a bit. She knows his faults better than anyone else. She ought to. She learned them first hand, by experience. He is as aware of them as she is and though he may never let on, he is very concerned about them. She may not have guessed it, but he marks himself down because of them. She knows all about him and still admires him. That makes her admiration significant.

He may have many male and even female friends who respect and encourage him, but no one has pledged the loyalty to him that you have offered. You are with him when he is riding high on success. You are with him when he is down. With everyone else he keeps up his guard to defend his weak spots, but he can relax with you. You know where he is vulnerable. You neither discredit him nor take advantage of this knowledge, except when you are playfully conniving for some little thing for yourself, your home or your children.

In fact he begins to rely on you to cover-up some of his inadequacies. As he grows confident of your respect, he will even let you help him improve on his deficiencies. If he doesn't have your respect-in-spite-of-what-he-is, he will begin to guard himself against you as well. You will be left wondering why there are barriers between you that never used to be there.

CHARGING THE BATTERY

A man may be challenged everywhere he goes. His ability, his authority, his manhood is continually challenged. There is always someone who can better him. Every man has times when he even doubts himself. He comes dragging home at night. His wife meets him and by her attitude to him lets him know that in her opinion he is the greatest guy in the world.

She re-charges his faltering battery, re-inflates his ego and re-affirms his confidence in himself. His psychological drive is renewed.

DRAINING THE BATTERY

Picture it the other way around. Maybe he feels respected everywhere but in his own home. Maybe he feels inferior everywhere. When he comes home he is met by his wife. Her tongue is armed with razor blades. With a few sharp words she cuts down whatever remains of his manhood. Nothing he does is right. Nothing he does will ever be right. Why can't he be like "Tom or Dick"? Nag. Nag. Nag.

He really gets it as she begins to unfavorably contrast him with all the other men in the neighborhood, with her father and her brothers. She couldn't hurt him more if she hit him between the legs with a baseball bat.

Emasculated

A man robbed of pride, dignity and self-esteem is a pitiful creature. He becomes defensive and withdrawn — often surly and resentful. He accepts defeat and gives up.

40

He may resort to alcohol or other escapisms. He may become impotent with further damage to his self-image.

He may try to mask his feelings with an exaggerated aggressiveness, grandiose schemes or sexual excess. He indulges in extra-marital relationships seeking to establish his virility. Feeling threatened he may become vile-tempered or abusive, most often toward those closest at hand, his wife and children.

He wants and needs his wife's respect more than he wants love or sex or status or money. He wants his wife to make him feel like he is a man — even when he acts like a boy.

ADMIRATION

This respect and admiration can be expressed in words. To carry any weight her words must be confirmed by her actions. It is best expressed by the relationship she has to her husband, the attitude she adopts toward him. The wife's attitude sets the tone for the entire household.

THE KING

This was clearly illustrated to a friend of mine who related a visit to the home of a casual acquaintance. She prepared to leave near supper hour. About 5:30 p.m. she noticed an excitement running through the household. Everything was in preparation for the husband's return. The mother told her children to pick up their toys, daddy would soon be home. The faces of the three children beamed at the mention of the father's return. The wife primmed herself. Father's anticipated arrival filled the house with joyful expectation. The excitement was obvious to the visitor. She gladly accepted an invitation to stay to supper as an opportunity to meet the man of the house. He must certainly be extra ordinary.

The door opened. The "King" had arrived and the entire court gave him full attention. A smiling wife and squealing children surrounded a very ordinary man — short of stature, uncomely, pre-maturely bald and dressed in the garb of a working man.

SUBMISSION

One of the characteristics of this relationship that shows the wife's respect is submission to her husband. More is written about submission elsewhere, but I will briefly state here that submission involves a voluntary yielding to the authority and leadership of another.

Picture it like this. Here is this lovely, intelligent, young lady. She has a job with a fair salary. She spends her money as she wishes. Her life is her own. She is free and independent. With a bit of extra effort and training she could make a career for herself. Maybe she already has everything she needs for a career.

Along comes Prince Charming. She surrenders her independence and freedom, alters her identity — even changing her name, to marry him. She takes a lot of extra work for which she will not be paid. If she continues to be gainfully employed, she puts much of her money toward paying his indebtedness for education, home and automobile. Her success or failure becomes linked to him. Much of her time, energy and ability is directed towards him and the children she bears to him. The direction of her life may take a vastly different course and she will have far less control over the new course than over the former.

Being an enquiring person, I ask myself — "Why did this beautiful, intelligent woman give up all that to marry me? Try as I will I can come up with only one logical answer. She gave up all that to marry me because I am such a great guy."

A man wants to be treated as if his wife believes he is the greatest guy in the world. They both know she is wrong, but that doesn't matter.

By her submission a wife continually demonstrates the respect she has for her husband. She voluntarily accepts his leadership, yields to his authority as an expression of confidence in him. She learns how to make him feel like he is someone special. She wouldn't have married him if she hadn't thought that of him in the first place. She demonstrates, by living out the relationship of a wife to her husband, that she still feels that way about him.

He comes home. Maybe he has had a hard, discouraging day, or maybe he's had a carefree, relaxed golf game. A lovely lady meets him at the door and acts as if his home coming was the greatest event of her day.

Keep pouring that sort of admiration into him. There won't be enough pins in the world to puncture his balloon.

DREAMS VS. REALITY

This is how you felt about him before you married him. In your dream, you were always going to feel that way. You weren't going to let your marriage deteriorate into the nagging, raging scenes you had witnessed in other marriages. You were never going to speak of, or to, your husband after the fashion of some of the disgruntled women you had heard.

You say he has changed since you married him. Ten to one any changes he had made are an improvement over his former self. You have just gotten to know him better. You know ... the hammer of time ... the anvil of reality ...

You wanted most of all to be loved. He

wanted to be respected. Now he has hurt you so often that as much as you'd like to be able to, you say you can't respect him. You confess that you must have been moonstruck. You hadn't known him well enough. You hadn't realized what you were getting yourself into.

That may be so. Your courtship assessment of your intended may have been unrealistic, but the One who inspired Paul to tell wives to submit to, obey and respect their husbands had no delusions about the sort of material husbands are made of. He commanded the respect just the same.

By the same token, He had no delusions about women when He commanded husbands to love their wives.

There are certain basic things that must be put into a marriage if it is to work. Each partner must make his or her respective contribution. When things are not going right, everyone of us is tempted to withdraw that contribution from the system.

FOOLISH

Three fools agreed together to buy an automobile. It was agreed that A would maintain the tires and ensure they were properly inflated. B was to see that there was always adequate gasoline in the tank, and C was to service the cooling and electrical systems.

One morning A went out to start the

automobile. It refused to start. The gas tank was completely empty. Enraged that B had failed to keep up his commitment, A slashed all the tires. C, coming along at that time was furious that both A and B were defaulting. He took a sledge hammer and smashed the radiator and battery. Venting his spleen still more he smashed the lights and windows and made huge dents in the body of the car.

Many couples treat their marriage as the three fools treated their automobile. There is no way you can improve your marriage by withdrawing your rightful contribution. That will in no way make up for your partner's deficiency. It will only make the situation worse.

Many couples are faced with the same decision confronting the three fools. Shall they repair that which has been damaged to a greater degree by their outbursts of anger, or shall they scrap it and lose everything they have invested in it?

You could string off his faults in a list a mile long. If you keep majoring on his faults, you will be able to lose all respect for him.

THE WISE

By and large, I don't countenance the criticisms brought against the King James Version, but I'm sure the translators must have made an error in addressing Philippians 4:8 to "brethren." It looks to me like it is taylor-made for wives.

" . . . whatsoever things are true, whatsoever things are honest, whatsoever things are just, whatsoever things are pure, whatsoever things are lovely, whatsoever things are of good report; if there be any virtue, and if there be any praise, THINK ON THESE THINGS."

Chapter 5

I LOVE YOU

A woman looks at this submission thing and says, "Okay, so I submit to my husband, I agree to obey him. What is there to stop him from abusing me? What protection do I have?"

That is a good question. What prevents the husband from exploiting his wife? What protection is there for the wife when she has submitted to the authority of her husband?

A PIECE OF CHATEL

The fact is many women are being exploited in their marriages. The relationship has deteriorated in many homes from love and submission to suppression and exploitation. There is a cry raised across the land that marriage is legalized rape, implying that in marriage the woman is held by contract to give to her husband whatever he demands while he is not held to give anything in return. She must make herself available to be used or abused at his will.

You have only to walk around with your eyes open to know that this happens. Various women's organizations have recognized this and are raising a protest. The protest is valid even if the motives of some protestors are questionable. For many of them the goal appears to be the destruction of marriage itself, rather than the correction of injustices found in many modern marriages.

Women have a right to dignity, decency, honor and respect, and they should receive these from their husbands more than from any other. The problem is not in marriage per se, nor does the Christian marriage foster the exploitation of women. The problem is not in the institution of marriage. Dissolving present marriages by divorce, and abolishing future marriages will not solve the problem.

THE HEART OF THE MATTER

The problem was identified hundreds of years ago. It is the hardness of heart, the cruelty with which a man will treat his wife.

The solution is a change of heart. The power to change is available to any who will ask.

The marriage ceremony didn't harden anyone's heart and abolishing it won't soften anyone. With or without marriage ceremonies, men and women will continue to get together and in some such unions the partners will be cruel to each other. As a result of this and other problems, some or even many of these unhappy unions will break up. This disruption of an intimate relationship causes emotional trauma. The couple who avoided a marriage ceremony are no less susceptible to this pain.

SHE COULD LEAVE

Women remain in an undesirable marriage, they stay in a relationship of suppression and exploitation not because it is too hard to break the contract nor because it costs too much money to get a divorce.

Most women who remain in an untenable situation do so because they believe in what they are trying to do. They believe in marriage, home and family. They are putting everything they have into it, because they believe in it. What is more they would consider themselves adequately rewarded if they could receive a bit of praise, love and appreciation from their husbands and their children.

CALCULATED RISK

Submission does expose one to the risk of exploitation. When a woman surrenders her independence and accepts a position under the authority of her husband, she makes herself vulnerable. She is subject to his misjudgements and exposed more than any other person to any mean streak in his personality.

She allows herself to be placed in that position only because she trusts him not to take advantage of her.

Her safeguard is in his character. No honorable man would willfully take advantage of those subject to his authority.

A woman would do well to select her husband on the basis of his character without so much emphasis on his looks or clothing or status or charm unless these latter are the things she values most highly.

Children are aware of their mother's sensitive position. They will try to defend her against the advantage of the father. They express a mixture of fear, anger and sorrow for the way "my dad treats my mom."

Children can teach us a lot if we would listen. One day we had a heated discussion at the breakfast table. I stood up, hit the table with my fist, and raised my voice to make a point. The discussion continued. There was a bit of commotion near me but I ignored it. Our little boy, Shane Douglas, five years old at the time, had pushed a chair toward me. Standing on it, with one little hand on my shoulder and the other over my open mouth, he said, with tears in his voice, "Please daddy, don't say it. Please, daddy, stop talking." By this time Shawna Dee was standing by her mother and joining in Donna's defense. My point may well have been correct, but I was acting incorrectly. Their father's anger was no greater than their mother's, yet they felt she was being threatened and they pleaded her defense.

DISARMED

Vulnerability is a risk both partners take. When you open your life to another person, expose your weaknesses, reveal your hidden feelings and thoughts; offer the most precious thing you have — that is your love, you are in effect taking off your armor. You are dismantling your defenses: defenses you built up over the years as protection against inner hurt. You stand naked; unprotected. You trust your partner not to betray the confidence you have demonstrated.

Just as you must slit the bark of a tree and press into it the fresh-cut end of a bud to produce a graft, so must man and woman open their lives to each other if they are to grow together as one.

NO STRINGS ATTACHED

The couple could enter marriage with all their defenses erect, approach each other encased in armored plating, their missles in firing position, an escape route carefully laid out.

Indeed many couples are seeking to protect themselves from the hazards and hurts of marriage by entering a relationship that is in fact not a marriage.

They commit themselves for as long as they feel love for each other.

They talk of trial marriages, propose renewable marriage contracts, ponder group marriages and participate in swinging relationships. They advocate a partnership in which the roles are identical, while the need is for roles that are different but complementary.

Such individuals may get their mail at the same address, eat at the same table, sleep in the same bed, copulate and procreate, but they are not married. They think they are free of the hurts and hazards of marriage because what they have is not a marriage.

The basic philosophy behind such innovations is comparable to the policy of not eating in order to avoid food poisoning.

It is true that the less one gives, the less one stands to lose. It is unlikely, however, that these people are in fact spared the hurt they seek to avoid.

When a temporary arrangement has fallen through, sleeping around anywhere and belonging nowhere leaves you empty, lonely and depressed.

Having invested nothing, the odds are entirely in favor of a similar profit. You will realize dividends of the same order — little or nothing.

Withdrawing to avoid further hurts, leaves you feeling much the same. This is not meant to imply that all those who remain single do so on a basis of fear or hurt. The decision to remain single is the prerogative of any man or woman and should not be looked upon with suspicion.

MOONLIGHT AND ROSES . . . AND THORNS

On the other hand, a couple may enter marriage with open honesty, love and trust; then taken aback by unexpected and usually unintentional hurts, not knowing how to handle the attendant problems of a growing relationship, they instinctively reconstruct their defenses and go to battle stations.

Have you ever walked into a home that was arrayed for battle? Donna and I lived like that for a number of years. We enjoyed temporary truces, but we never really disarmed our warheads or dismantled our defenses. Constantly on guard we were ready to explode at the slightest provocation. We were super-sensitive to the most innocent remark. We tried hard and usually succeeded in keeping up a good front before the community. There is no benefit to hanging all your dirty linen on a public clothes line. Nevertheless, secret strife leaves you as far from the goal as public warfare or divorce.

The safeguard is interwoven with the instruction that calls for submission. The scriptures that teach the wife to submit, to be subject to, to reverence her husband, give instruction to the husband in triplicate to love his wife; to love her as Christ loved the church; to love her as his own body; to love her as himself.[1]

He loves her. He may be aware of her weakened bargaining position, but he responds by upholding her with love preferring that to using her selfishly for his own profit.

HE LOVES HER

Those of us who watch movies and read romance novels know what love is. It is a hug and a kiss and off to bed. It is a powerful feeling that explodes inside two people when the vibrations are right. Enamored with each other, this feeling "lifts" them over any problems or obstacles and leaves them floating like fleecy white

---

1. Ephesians 5:22-31

clouds in the blue sky. Somehow there is the mystical faith that if they can just keep the feeling going they will be spared the problems that shake ordinary marriages.

What is love? What is a young man talking about when he tells a young lady that he loves her? What is he talking about when he asks her to prove her love to him? What is a mother talking about when she says she loves her baby? A lady sits in my office and says there is no more love in their marriage. She says she can't love her husband anymore. What is she talking about? People talk about making love. What are they talking about?

Most people talking about love are talking about a feeling. Love has feeling. It has a wonderful feeling.

The Greeks had four words for our one word love. They spoke of *EROS*. This is physical love. We use a similar word "erotic" to describe sexual love or sexual stimulation. Perhaps it is well expressed by the word passion.

PHILIA is the love of people, brotherly love, the love between friends, the steadfast love or affection that comes from the experience of facing life together, from having a unity of purpose, a love apart from passion.

A third word *STORGE* describes the love of a child for a parent, of a brother for a sister, a love into which sex does not enter at all.

The fourth word *AGAPE* means spiritual love or God's love. It is the love that reaches out in goodwill even to the one who has hurt you.

Religious people particularly have a tendency to eulogize brotherly love and spiritual love while treating the subject of erotic love with silent embarrassment. The latter is a rather strange position for a Christian to hold. The Christian's God takes the credit for creating sex.

He made them male and female. That is sex. Sexual desire is a natural function. Passion is a perfectly normal human emotion. The desire of the man for the woman and of the woman for the man is perfectly proper and normal. There is no reason for shame in the desire they have for each other.

The desire for sexual love requires discipline in its expression. Combined with other aspects of love it is a marvelous symbol of the unity between a husband and wife and is indeed a unifying force between them. Apart from the other aspects of love, or divorced from any continuing responsibility to the sexual partner, sexual intercourse becomes an exercise in self-love and is no more conducive to sound relationships than any other act of selfishness.

Immorality, wantonness, guilt, uncleanness are not involved in the desire alone. Young people sometimes become aware of their passion with a sense of fear and guilt. Many older folk still struggle with the guilt they absorbed in youth when their attitudes were being shaped in the era of silent embarrassment.

Men, however, are quite physical in their concept of love and most men will engage their wives in sexual love without being pushed. More often this is an area of problem for the women. A woman is just as capable of passion, but to her being loved means much more than going to bed.

LOVE IS TREATMENT

To a woman love is more than an emotion. It is treatment.

A woman knows she is loved by the way she is treated. A woman is assured of her husband's love not by the frequency of trips to the bedroom, but by the way he treats her between trips. If he would treat her with love, she just might race him to the bedroom rather than throw up road blocks on the way.

To a woman love is kindness, gentleness, understanding, praise, private and public demonstration that her husband is pleased with her. She will respond more easily to your private affection when there has been some public counterpart to it. I don't mean that you rehearse the bedroom scene at the dinner party, but when you go with your wife to a gathering of people, don't ignore her all evening. Give her some of your attention. If you are not sitting together at the function, look at her once in awhile. When you have the opportunity, sit with her for awhile. Talk to her.

It seems socially accepted and expected that in public a man plays the role of the virile stud talking and acting flirtatious with everyone else's wife while ignoring his own. The women are likewise expected to play their part in the game. If they do speak of or to each other, it must be to make little digs in semi-derogatory remarks. This is classified as clever and witty. Such may be socially accepted but they are at best jokes in poor taste and a bad habit that quickly becomes destructive.

Love includes being treated with politeness, courtesy, dignity, honesty, justice and fairness. Have you ever thought of treating your wife with courtesy? Politeness and graciousness are too often reserved for people outside the home.

A friend related a story about two of his children. One day they were playing outside. The boy, a bit older than his sister, was bullying her. A passerby stopped and asked the boy, "Is that any way to treat a lady?" The boy replied, "She's not a lady. She's my sister." The implication being "that gives me the right to treat her any way I want."

In the earlier years of our marriage, Donna and I went one evening to a dinner meeting. As was increasingly frequent at that time, we had left the house quarreling and driven in vile humor to the dinner. On arrival we concealed the hatchet temporarily. I sat at the head table mentally honing the hatchet to a fine edge. I would be ready when we returned home. I was sitting to the right of the guest speaker. He was talking to the man on his left and obviously referring to his own marriage at sometime in the past. I overheard two sentences. He said "God rebuked me. 'What right do you have to treat the lady I gave you that way?' "

I applied that thought to my own marriage and said within myself, "She is my wife. I'll treat her anyway I want." But it started me thinking.

Up to that time and for some time after it really never occurred to me I treated Donna badly. Who would have ever thought to apply I Corinthians 13 to a marriage partner anyway?

LISTEN AND LEARN

We come to marriage without prior experience. We have a general idea of how a husband and wife treat each other, but we can't apply all the generalities to the specific individual we marry. The treatment has to be individualized. No one is better able to tell you how your wife wants to be treated, *than your wife herself.* Little things that are innocent to you may be offensive to her. A mole hill to you may be a mountain to her and vice-versa. Unless husband and wife talk to each other about their feelings, they cannot know how the other feels about specific things and will often be left bewildered by the reaction of one partner to something that appears innocuous to the other.

When you learn that something offends your spouse, however innocent it is to you, love demands a modification of your action, or at least a careful explanation.

PRAISE

A woman wants her husband's approval. To her this also is love. To be approved, she must meet his expectations. If his expectations are too high for her to attain, she will continually fall short. His excessive demands are seen as a lack of concern for her. If he loved her he wouldn't put such a heavy load on her.

OVER BURDENED

A woman will judge her husband unloving if he leaves her with too much of the burden of the home and fails to take his proper responsibility in training and disciplining the children and in maintaining order in the home. A woman is designed to be a helper not a replacement for a man.

She knows for sure he doesn't love her when having left her all the burden of the home, he then turns and condemns her for the problems that arise.

THE CHILLY VALLEY

A man can become very affectionate, when he starts to feel the urge. At such time he could charm a picture off the wall. After his passion has been satisfied he can return to acting as if his wife doesn't even exist. He may not give her the time of day until his appetite grabs him again.

Some husbands can be downright mean between passion plays, irritable, critical, demanding, indifferent. Some carry their meanness into the sexual act. Love gives way to legalized rape.

A woman's capacity to enjoy the climb up passion heights is every bit as great as a man's. There is one difference though. She is much more sensitive to the chill of the valley. It is not surprising that, after a time, a woman may say to her husband, "There was a time I enjoyed climbing the mountain with you, but the valley experience between the peaks is too cold. Going up only makes the coming down more painful. I don't want to go mountain climbing anymore."

At this point, the husband brings his wife to the doctor and says, "Fix her up, Doc. She's frigid."

I'm not defending women who close their bedroom door to their husbands. If there are problems in the marriage already, the most foolish thing in the world for a woman to do is to send her husband out of the house feeling like a young stallion.

LOVE MAKING

It is just that women find it difficult to fight all day, give and take abuse, then crawl into bed, forget it all, and make love.

Making love doesn't start after you are in bed at night. *It starts when you get up in the morning. It is the treatment you give your wife all day long.*

In marriage the thing most important to the woman is love. In return for love she will give her all to the home, her husband and her family and find fulfillment in so doing.

Love is her security. She is married to you. She has become socially, emotionally and probably financially dependent on you. She placed herself in jeopardy when she gave up her independence and linked herself to you.

Granted, she didn't want to be independent. She didn't want to be the last link in the chain, the last resource in every crisis. She wanted to be linked to a supportive man. She wanted what marriage had to offer and recognized the risks. The assurance of your love convinced her to accept the risks with confidence.

You assured her you loved her. She placed confidence in you. Your love is the continuing safeguard that you won't betray her trust.

Now you have some children. She wants her children to have a father, a home, food, clothes, and an education. She has become increasingly more dependent. Yet what hold does she have on you? What is there to stop you from leaving the house some morning and never coming back? She may be able to go after you for some support, but she wants and needs much more than money.

She watches you go away in the morning. Maybe these thoughts have never presented themselves or her conscious mind, but down inside whe knows the only hold she has on you, the only guarantee you will come home, is your love. You will continue caring for her because you love her. Her security, the security of everything she holds dear is wrapped-up in you and your love. It is no wonder she wants continuing reassurance of your love.

Some man says, "The silly goose should know I love her. I told her so twenty years ago on our honeymoon."

She is secure, confident of your love, a confidence confirmed by the way you treat her.

I am convinced that eighty percent of the women on tranquilizers could be taken off their medication if, let's say three times a week — you wouldn't want to do it too often, it would blow their minds — the husband would come into the house, put his arms around his wife, kiss her and without ulterior motives say, "I love you!"

I will not try to list the services the average woman gives to the home. Few men could afford to pay for such service if they went out to hire it. The one payment she really wants is her husband's love. The miserable skinflint she married is ten years behind in his payments. What payment he does make hardly takes care of the interest let alone the principle.

I wanted to give something really great
    for you
But God out-did me, he made the sky so
    blue

I wanted to give something shining and
    bright
But God out-did me, he made the sun and
    gave us light.

I wanted to give you something full of joy
    and mirth
But God out-did me, he made the earth.

I couldn't find anything as great as the
    things from above
Then God said, "Equal me and give her
    love."

So I thank God for the sky so blue
But most of all I thank God for you.

Cole Ahnefeld

Chapter 6

THE HEAD

For the husband is the head of the wife even as Christ is the head of the church (Ephesians 5:23).

I would have you know that the head of every man is Christ and the head of the woman is the man . . . (I Corinthians 11:3).

Unto the woman he said . . . your desire shall be to your husband, and he shall rule over you (Genesis 3:16).

LEADERSHIP

The subject, "The Head," is a discussion on leadership. A leader or ruler is one who governs. To govern means to control, manage or direct. The leader or the head of a system is one who ensures that guidance and direction is given to that system.

In the total process of leadership,

authority may be delegated to, and shared by, a number of people. In most situations it is imperative that authority be invested in more than one individual or the absence of that one will lead to a total breakdown in direction. It is equally important that within the chain of command there is someone, who, operating within certain limits, has final decision-making authority. If this concept is not practiced, disagreement within the leadership will lead to stalemate, indecisiveness and again to a breakdown in direction.

SURVIVAL THROUGH LEADERSHIP

The leadership of the home is invested in both father and mother. Children are instructed to obey their parents; plural.[1] To the children, father and mother are both figures of authority. The instruction to obedience is given with the implication that respect for leadership is a safeguard to their survival, thus the expression "that your days may be long on the earth."

The lack of leadership or a voluntary detachment from leadership, that is rebellion, is detrimental to the function of any system. Even rebels look for someone to lead them in their rebellion. Anarchists invest authority in and accept guidance from a philosophy. One of the strangest

---

1. Ephesians 6:1-4; Colossians 3:20

things I have seen reported in a newspaper was that report several years ago of a delegate to the International Congress of Anarchists being thrown out of a conference for not respecting the order of the meeting.

Both parents and, in practice, older children as well, contribute to the leadership of the home, yet one person occupies the chief place. The scripture gives that place to the man. In the care of a home and the rearing of children he is given an assistant. Not one to whom he relegates all the drudgery, but one who is elevated to a position beside him. He is not the only authority, but he is the final authority. He is the head.

As a boy on my father's farm I learned a fair bit of the importance of a head. I could tell which way one of my father's cattle were going by looking at its head. I never saw anything that didn't have a head go anywhere. I knew nothing at that time of the anatomy of the central nervous system but on Saturday afternoon when a young rooster lost his head on the chopping block, I knew the rest of him would be in the frying pan on Sunday.

Without a head the entire body loses its viability. The home, the family is an essential institution but it is being destroyed for want of leadership. If a man is to be respected as the head in the home, it is imperative, it is absolutely imperative that he earns that respect. He cannot *demand* respect. He must *command* respect. While I firmly believe that poor government is better than no government all, it is mighty difficult to encourage people to respect authority when those occupying the position of authority act in an irresponsible manner.

THE ESSENCE OF LEADERSHIP

When we talk about the head we are talking about authority, the right to command, leadership. What is the essence of leadership?

PRIVILEGE?

As I listen to remarks made by people wanting equality, I get the impression that the majority are referring to equal privilege or equal status. It is true that position and privilege comes with leadership.

In our dining room there is one chair with arm rests. It is called the captain's chair. It marks the head of the table. That is where I sit. Donna sits in the first mate's chair. Sometimes I would put our young son in my chair. He would say "How come I's sittin' in the capun's chair?" The chair is nothing in itself, but it is symbolically meaningful provided that which it represents in symbol exists in fact.

70

RESPONSIBILITY

The essence of leadership, however, is not privilege. It is responsibility. Privilege and position are rewards *earned* through accepting and discharging responsibility.

THE BOARD OF INQUIRY

When the graceful destroyer escort returns to harbor, its flags fluttering in the breeze and a welcoming band assembled on the jetty, every man on board ship would love to be the captain.

The ship ties up along side. The brow is lowered. The captain is piped ashore. Every woman waiting on the jetty to welcome her husband home, would be so proud if her man were the captain.

Then when you hear the sickening sound of gravel scraping on the keel, every man back on board ship thanks God he was passed over in the last promotion list. The lower his position, the more likely it is that he will go home untroubled while the captain dances on the carpet in front of the board of inquiry.

For whatever reason, in marriage the man has been placed in the chief place, the position of ultimate leadership. He manifests this leadership, not by exacting privilege and running roughshod over the other members, but by exercising concern for the welfare of every individual under him, including his second-in-command, and by directing the family unit toward its goals. This requires provision of more than food and clothing.

You are not in a position of privilege; you are in a position of responsibility. You are ultimately responsible for the welfare of the family. If a corporation becomes bankrupt you don't place the blame on the shareholders, though they suffer loss as well as the executives. The responsibility is placed squarely at the feet of the president.

The objective of the family is to provide essential supportive care for each member; to prepare the children to live in *their* future world and to provide an environment where each person, adult and child, can develop as an individual; where each develops the sense of being a person in his or her own right yet maintains identity with, expresses loyalty for and makes contribution to the family group.

Come off your perch, Pop. You have a role in life that is much better fitted with humility. The paramount issue is not to occupy the throne. The essential is to provide leadership in your castle. If you are going to succeed you will have to give *yourself* to it.

I do not fault marriage itself, but would offer that one major fault in marriage today is that the husband has maintained the status traditionally offered in marriage, has accepted the privilege so offered, but has defaulted in the obligation he owes his household. One pressing social problem is the irresponsible father — the sort of man who (before the advent of The Pill) was home often enough to keep his wife pregnant. The pill hasn't improved on him but it has spared his wife somewhat.

MUTUAL BENEFITS

Now don't get frightened, Father. I'm not describing a one-way street where you give everything and get nothing. The ship that the captain keeps afloat, also keeps the crew afloat. The members of your family, however, have needs that must be met. You are responsible to see that those needs are met. The early Christian church taught that a man who did not provide for those of his own household had denied the faith and was worse than an infidel.[1]

A WELFARE CHEQUE

I'm sorry, Father, I can't let you off with simply providing physical needs. Your family has needs in addition to food and shelter. It is tragic that the contributions many men make to the home could be replaced entirely by a welfare cheque.

A man who is away from the home for

---

1. Timothy 5:8

long periods or for many hours each day should make it a point to give *himself* to his family when he is home. Some men find it hard to give themselves. In a semi-detached way they can provide finances, correction and so on, but remain emotionally distant. *You are responsible to see that your children are provided with the necessary love, warmth, instruction and discipline.* They require personal, parental guidance and at the same time a graduated liberation to allow development of their own sense of direction.

You may enlist the help of the school, church and clubs to assist you in providing these things, but you cannot abdicate your responsibility. I think we need to ask ourselves, "What is the home, the school, the church doing to help our children prepare themselves to successfully live the life ahead of them?"

THE CROWN IS GETTING HEAVY

You are the head. How well the ancient barb has said "Uneasy lies the head that bears the crown." You are responsible. What does that mean in everyday events?

Does it mean you have to have all the answers?

Does it mean the only valid opinion on any subject is your opinion?

Does it mean you personally make all the decisions?

Does it mean you never make a mistake and most certainly never admit to one?

Does it mean you must personally be the resource to meet every need and to solve every problem?

I suspect many men approach marriage this way. Somehow a glimmer of the message came through that being head meant taking responsibility. This seems to mean they have to have all the answers, be the sole voice of authority on every subject. They know they don't possess these qualities but it seems to be expected and they are going to play the part come hell or high water.

THE TYRANT

Any suggestion that you are not all-wise, all-knowing, all-sufficient, is taken as a challenge to your shaky throne and must be met head on with brute force and rage before it has a chance to topple you. The suggestion is most likely to come from the ones you are playing the superman game with, that is Mrs. Solomon and the children. For this reason a man who is quite normal and pleasant outside the home may become a critical, oppressive tyrant in the home as he tries vainly to stamp out any evidence that he is not all he thinks he is supposed to be. To allow someone else to contribute in the area of your weaknesses would be an admission to the weaknesses, so you ridicule their attempts to help. If you can make them look really stupid, perhaps by contrast you will look a little better.

Anything other family members do is ridiculed, particularly if they do it better than father can do it. Father competes with everyone and forces everyone to compete with him, then sitting in the judge's seat gives himself first prize and shoots everyone else down in flames. If father plays the role well, the household may buy it. The children grow up believing father is a veritable colossus and each of them by contrast a blithering idiot. If, however, father plays the game poorly, the household sees through him and disintegrates with smoldering resentment.

THE DEFAULTER

Some men take the opposite tack. They accept the fanciful delusion that they are supposed to be equal with God but realize they are not. Rather than continue the masquerade they throw in the towel, abdicate the throne, abandon the ship and let the entire burden fall on the wife. The wife taxed beyond capacity resents the unreasonable burden. She loses respect for her defaulting husband. The children following her lead suffer the same loss of respect for father and subsequently are hindered in the development of their own self-respect.

PARENTAL RESPECT:
SELF RESPECT

You cannot despise the clay and esteem the pottery made from it. The commandment to honor your parents[1] is not given to protect the ancestors. It is a safeguard for the descendants. One of the frequent tragedies in marital strife is that one embittered member of the relationship poisons the minds of the children against the other member. It is difficult, if not impossible, for a child to learn to love himself, if he grows up hating his parents.

DOUBLE LOSER

Some men play parts of both games. Like the dictator, they suppress any other expression of leadership. Like the defaulter they renege on their responsibility. The ship runs aground. The captain won't pull it off the rocks and forbids anyone else to try.

Many homes face leadership crisis. There is a reason for the dilemma and there is a solution.

---

1. Exodus 20:12; Deuteronomy 5:16; Matthew 15:4; 19:19; Mark 7:10; 10:19; Luke 18:20; Ephesians 6:2.

DILEMMA

You have been given the responsibility to see that the job is done, but you don't have the capability. That seems a bit unfair doesn't it? It doesn't seem right to place responsibility on a man without giving him the ability to carry it out.

THE SOLUTION

That imperfect and less-than-totally-adequate man, loaded with responsibility, could be given a helper to assist him in his task.

It's coming through. That's right. Open your eyes, you big dummy, she's sitting right there across the room from you. You have finally grasped what God realized a long time ago. You need a helper.

You don't know it all and you aren't expected to but you are expected to make use of the help God has given you.

She's lovely and she is sexy but she wasn't designed to be a sex symbol or a status symbol. She was designed to be a helper. You need her and she needs you. So get over your superman complex, stop trying to play God, come down to earth and start working together as a team.

If she is to help you she must be given appropriate authority. I have come to believe in the inspiration of the scriptures but I don't believe the hard-bitten interpretation that some people place on the scriptures. Some have misinterpreted scripture to justify male suppression of women. A woman's role is not that of a slave. Women share in the exercise of authority.

God gave the man and the woman preeminence over the rest of His creation.[1] He told *them* to have dominion and authority. I don't say He gave them equal authority but He gave it to *them together.*

The husband is not the sole source of leadership in the home. If he were the home would fall apart in his frequent absences. In fact, the scripture does *NOT* say that the husband is the head of the house. He is declared to be the head of the *woman.*[2]

Both husband and wife share in the leadership of the home. As stated before, children are commanded to obey both parents, to recognize both of them as figures of authority. As a household grows, others are included in the leadership. Domestic employees, baby-sitters and older children, in various circumstances, are given appropriate authority to ensure continuous leadership in the temporary absence of both parents. It need not be in absence only. Employees can be, and older children should be given graduated authority and

---

1. Genesis 1:28.
2. Ephesians 5:23; I Corinthians 11:3.

allowed to share in the care, and responsibility of the household.

From the time Shawna Dee was six years old she involved herself in the care of her little brother. She was eight years old when we travelled with them halfway around the world. By simply allowing her to do so she made his safety her responsibility. Through crowded airports and train depots, I watched over the luggage, Donna kept her eye on Shawna Dee who in turn guarded Shane. He could not have escaped her with the help of a dozen paid assistants. Even now she admonishes us that his training is far in arrears in several important areas.

The man and his wife share the authority in the home. When there is a difference of opinion, one is given the edge over the other to facilitate decision-making. That extra edge of authority is placed at the husband's end of the table. He is her head.

THE LIBERATED WOMAN

The position of the husband as head of the wife has significance that reaches far beyond decision-making. It is a quiet reminder to the children, to domestic employees, to guests and indeed to all the world that if you intend to challenge this woman you had better prepare to do battle with the man who stands behind her. He is her head. She acts under his authority. If you challenge her, you are automatically in confrontation with him.

His position is her safeguard. She is free to give herself to her household and to her husband, to plan, to counsel, to create and innovate without having to dissipate energy building her own defenses. She operates under the umbrella of his authority. It doesn't suppress her. It liberates her.

No woman can be liberated in her marriage, until her husband will accept and fulfill the responsibility of leadership — and until she has submitted to that leadership.

Women campaigning against masculine leadership in the home (campaigning to have their heads removed) are working against their own best interest.

FULFILLED THROUGH SHARING

A man is not demeaned by sharing authority with his wife. One of the qualities admired in a leader is the willingness to delegate authority and responsiblity to those under him and to allow them to develop their skills, the exercise of which accrues as much to his credit as to theirs.

The man should not plan to handle every situation and make every decision. He should look for the person most capable to do the job. The man who recognizes his wife's superior ability in some area and utilizes that ability is not abdicating his position as head. He is using his head.

What a blessed thing it is if he is man enough to recognize his weakness and her strength and to capitalize on her strength rather than subject them both to his particular weakness.

Only a foolish woman would use her superior ability in some such area to discredit her husband. Indeed this seldom happens. There is far more ill feeling that comes as a result of a husband stubbornly bungling along, callously rejecting his wife's offers of assistance and discrediting her ability in an effort to boost his failing ego.

Few women wish to compete with their husbands for leadership. They do, however, want to be considered as intelligent creatures and they want to be allowed to make a meaningful, intelligent contribution to the family. They have come to the marriage wanting to contribute. They deserve to be credited with the ability they have, encouraged and praised in its use. Many husbands would be surprised to learn how desperately their wives desire to please them. Some women have given-up trying because their efforts have been treated with disdain.

It is a leaders duty to determine the abilities of his subordinates and make best use of these abilities for the over-all welfare of the system.

Let's say, for instance, there is a financial problem in the home. The husband realizes that his wife is a more thrifty person than himself. He turns the finances over to her. She handles the money — pays bills, budgets and so on. He has not reneged on his responsibility. He is making wise use of his resources. The fact she handles the money doesn't mean she has usurped his authority. She is simply performing a task he gave her, providing a service required for the welfare of the whole family.

He cannot wash his hands of the matter. She must have access to him to discuss the problems she meets in carrying out the task he gave her. He must be prepared to make allowance for her mistakes and must still accept ultimate responsibility for the matter. If mistakes are made he must correct them, but in correcting an error he must also recognize and praise the desire she had to please and to assist him.

Blessed is the man who gives his praise in public and his correction in private.

Chapter 7

SUBMISSION

... Your desire shall be to your husband
and he shall rule over you (Genesis 3:16).

Wives submit yourselves unto your own
husbands as unto the Lord (Ephesians
5:22; Colossians 3:18).

Let ... the wife see that she reverence
her husband (Ephesians 5:33).

Likewise you wives be in subjection to
your own husbands ... (I Peter 3:1).

For after this manner, in the old time,
the holy women also, who trusted in God,
adorned themselves, being in subjection
unto their own husbands (I Peter 3:5).

MALE CHAUVINISM

When first read by a modern person and
left standing by themselves, the above
statements could well be dismissed as the

rantings of a male chauvinist, a put down on women, a manifesto designed to suppress women in a male-dominated world.

Perhaps much of the problem in the traditional marriage is that these statements have been left standing by themselves, and used to promote an unreasonable inequality between men and women.

There are still some men who hold women in contempt. For them it needs to be pointed out that the total expression of scripture paints a picture of an equality between man and woman. They are both special creations; both are included in the plan of redemption; both are children of God. There is neither Jew nor Greek, there is neither bond nor free, there is neither male nor female, for you are all one in Christ Jesus.[1]

Both are given the responsibility to subdue the earth and govern it and every living thing.[2] Women cannot be totally excluded from any part of the arena of human activity. They may well major in some areas, but they have a part to play in all.

EQUAL BUT DIFFERENT

This equality is not synonymous with similarity. Some women regret their

---

1. Galations 3:28
2. Genesis 2:28

womanhood and seek a false equality best described as a desire for masculine similarity. To whatever extent one may emphasize their equality, one must recognize man and woman are not the same.

They are different and different in such a way that they complement one another. They have joint involvement in bringing the same tasks to completion, but their roles are different yet complementary.

If one is to provide leadership in the home, the complementary role is submission. There cannot be leadership without submission to the authority of the leader.

It is true that a man makes himself a leader by leading. It is equally true that others make him a leader by following.

There is no great threat to leadership when the youngest child in the family bucks authority, but leadership becomes improbable when the second-in-command is insubordinate.

I'm saying that wives have a large part to play in making their husbands the head of the family. Likewise, many wives who complain of the failure of their husbands to provide leadership must accept much of the responsibility for that failure.

If you want leadership in your home you must lead the rest of the family in submitting to that leadership.

I expect husbands will get a lot of mileage out of the last two paragraphs. They were, however, written exclusively for the wives. If your husband is giving you trouble, have him go back and re-read Chapter Six.

A FALSE IMAGE

One of the difficulties in discussing leadership and submission, is the erroneous mental images that flash onto the screen when these words are spoken.

If leadership is viewed as synonymous with tyranny, the head or the leader will be looked upon as an unenlighted despot, a bigot and an oppressor of the disadvantaged. If submission is pictured as synonymous with suppression, speaking of a woman being submitted to her husband will bring to mind a woman wearing on her neck the marks of her husband's hobnailed boots.

SUBMISSION NOT SUPPRESSION

The word submission is often painted to make it look like suppression, yet these two words are poles apart in meaning.

Women do not fear submission. They fear suppression.

Much of the present resentment, frustration and confusion over male and female roles in marriage would be eliminated if both husband and wife understood submission and the husband refused any opportunity for suppression.

Whether intentionally or through ignorance, much of the current talk on liberation centers on the concept that leadership is tyranny, submission is suppressive and true liberty is the freedom to do one's own thing, to follow one's own feelings without regard for any authority higher than one's own self.

That latter concept has a fair chance of working in a society of one person. When you expand your society to include a mate and, further yet, to include your offspring, your concept of leadership, submission and liberty will have to change unless you are prepared to believe that in a multiple society there is only one person who really counts. The idea is "I will do my thing and let the rest make out the best they can."

I have endeavored in Chapter Six to develop a concept of leadership as a benevolent authority assuming broad responsibility for those under it.

When we begin to talk of women being submitted to their husbands, I recognize that immediately the word brings into the minds of most people a picture of something entirely different. The mental picture is of a browbeaten woman, a pitiful creature, robbed of personality, stripped of individuality, her creativity stifled, her originality shackled, her self-expression forbidden, left to be a doormat under some man's hard heel.

I acknowledge that this condition exists

in some houses, but this is not a description of a submitted woman. This is a picture of suppression.

Let me repeat a former statement. Women do not fear submission. They fear suppression. The difference depends largely on the husband and how he uses his position of authority.

POWER-CLOAKED IN GENTLENESS

A gentle breeze fills the sail and carries the boat to its destination. A wind unleashed in all its fury destroys everything in its path.

Hydroelectric power disciplined by transformers and circuit breakers safely illuminates most of the homes on this continent. Without these controls electrical power would destroy everyone in contact with it.

How many children and wives wish father could be wired with a fifteen amp circuit breaker? They might still get a jolt once in awhile, but with much less danger of electrocution.

A small bit of nuclear fuel regulated in the release of its energy heats boilers and drives turbine generators or motors with marvellous benefit. The explosion of the same fuel could destroy whole cities.

Who would not fear to be in the epi-centre of an earthquake, or in the path of a tidal wave. No one wants to bear the brunt of unbridled power. The qualities of gentleness, loving concern and benevolence brings a control to the husband in the use of his authority. He leads. He does not suppress. She is submitted. She is not destroyed.

SUBMISSION IS VOLUNTARY

There cannot be a leader without a follower. In submission one volunteers to follow. It is an exercise of choice and of free will.

It is the product of strength and freedom. True submission demands more courage and strength of character than the rebel has dreamed is possible. Rebellion in the defense of self-interest can be found in the smallest child. Submission is a non-optional principle of life that can be acquired only through a process of development and maturation. It applies in the home, in the school, in the community and in the nation.

COERCION

Suppression comes of coercion. You follow along with one arm twisted behind your back and a club over your head.

Repeatedly the scripture states that the man is the head of the woman, yet not once is he commanded to *make* her submit. He is commanded to *love* her.

If the Christian marriage advocated the

suppression of women by their husbands, then women's liberation would be the answer. Liberation, however, requires more than the removal of suppression.

LIBERTY

Remove suppression and you may bring people into liberty, but not necessarily, for liberty does not exist by itself. For everyone of us, freedom exists only in conjunction with that which is right and proper. Liberty is not the right to do what I want. It is the power to do what is right.

ANARCHY

If, on the other hand, the Christian marriage advocates submission of wives to their husbands and you remove this submission, you have not produced liberty. You have produced anarchy. When you have removed the concept of submission, you have not brought the home into freedom. You have lifted it off its foundation and put it on skids, heading it downhill to inevitable destruction.

Mother discards the authority of father. The children are only too glad to fllow suit. They take a page out of her book and reject the authority of both father and mother. The parents do not work in harmony. Mother has not enhanced father's authority and it is not there when she needs to draw on it to strengthen her own position.

LEARNED — NOT NATURAL

Submission is learned and is best learned by example. Rebellion comes naturally. Having no example to follow, the children learn nothing of submission. They have not been liberated. Removed from the authority that could have saved them from themselves, they become their own worst enemies.

Many a little boy has packed his most precious possessions; a smooth stone, a piece of colored glass, a knife that has lost its edge, a fish line and hook, rubber boots and a bent coin, then carefully printed a note to his mother, and with or without a knapsack tied to the end of a pole, has left the injustices of home, left the world of tooth brush, comb and soap in a mad dash for freedom.

After a bit of distance and in a short space of time, a different emotion fills this boy's heart. The hoot of an owl, a pang of hunger, a chilly wind, the awareness of being alone sends him scurrying home.

Some have seen the fear in that boy's little heart, have seen a parallel fear in the lives of adults and have concluded that such people have not the courage to be free.

Let's look at the little boy again. Was the

boy about to discover true liberty as he left his parent's door? As he retraced his steps was he turning away from freedom, or was he returning to freedom; freedom that could not be found outside the safety of his home?

Little people grow into big people and some of them repeat the same mad dash for freedom at a time when they are too big to return home and at a time when it is too late for them to learn what they needed to prepare them for life as adults.

Perhaps they lacked a warm, benevolent figure of authority that could have paved the way for them to give submission; perhaps they lacked a living lecture, taught by example, that would have demonstrated this principle; perhaps of their own volition or under the influence of pseudo-liberators, they have discarded as outdated and irrelevant lessons once learned.

I see such young people weekly when I examine them on intake into a local correctional institution. Only an archdeceiver would try to persuade you these people are free. They lost their freedom, not when they stood before the judge, but when they lost the incentive to accept authority and lost the courage to submit to that which is right and proper.

As each individual goes his own way, a law unto himself, doing his own thing, unlearned in discipline, he is of no use to the family group and tragically of no use to

94

himself. Run this statement through again using the feminine instead of the masculine gender and you come to the same end.

I have related elsewhere an incident in our family's affairs when I felt I had to say no to the combined wishes of Donna and the children. That was the time Shane informed me, "What right do you have to say no? You are not the boss around here."

Shawna Dee didn't say anything. She waited to see what would happen. When she returned home from school that day Donna told her, "We are going to do what your father thinks best."

My daughter's reply was full of reproach. "Did you give in to him? Don't you know you have a right to your own opinion? Don't you know God made the woman from the man's side to be his equal, not from his foot to be walked over?"

Already she had picked up the impression that deferring to another was cowtowing, that submission was suppressive.

"You are a person in your own right." That is correct, but the conclusion, you have a right to go your own way, is incorrect.

As a citizen of a nation, as a practicing member of the medical profession, as a motorist that uses the freeway, I understand authority and the benefit of submitting to it. In using the freeway, for example, we have freedom so long as we all obey the rules of the road. One motorist doing his own thing jeopardizes everyone's freedom. With everyone doing his own thing, there is no longer liberty on the freeway. There is only bedlam and destruction.

Have you noticed that people will regulate the fires in their furnaces, control the electricity that comes into their homes and will operate their automobiles with care and yet live their lives with abandon? What a curious new twist to materialism. Things are important, so we protect these with controls, but people are not important so we encourage the removal of all controls, load them on board a coach car deceptively labelled LIBERTY and start them off downhill bent for destruction.

HARMONY IN DIFFERENCE

Children learn submission, not by lectures, but by observing it in operation. They may have the fortune of learning that one can think differently from the leader and still be in harmony with his leadership, that one can pull with vigor in a given direction when one's own choice would have been to go a different way.

Suppression would leave a woman browbeaten and incapable of individual thought or self-expression. Submission leaves her capable of using her own mind, able to formulate her own opinions and free to express them. Yet when her counsel is not followed and the course is finally set in a different direction than she would have taken, submission means that she supports the decision as enthusiastically as if it had been her own. She knows the ship has a better chance of surviving a misjudgment than it has of surviving mutiny. The rest of the crew follow her example.

What happens when it turns out that she was right in the first place and the captain has erred? She discreetly seals her lips, quietly gets out her paddle and helps pull the boat off the rocks.

What happens when the captain follows the advise of his first-mate and the ship runs aground? He recognizes that his wife's counsel was given out of a sincere desire for the welfare of the entire family. He humbly remembers that whatever the source of the counsel, the final decision was his responsibility. He loudly praises her motives and quietly corrects the error.

Well, I promised you a look at a submitted wife. The picture is found in the Resource Book that laid the foundation for our traditional marriage.[1] This is not the picture of a woman whose role in marriage has degraded and beaten her into a colorless shell of humanity. This is not the picture of a non-entity, ground into the

---

1. Proverbs 31:10-31

dirt. This is the picture of a vital, capable person, very much in touch with things and very much a somebody in her own right.

Proverbs Chapter Thirty-One describes a trustworthy, industrious and competent administrator. She is an expert purchasing agent. She handles real estate transactions. She is skilled in performing the tasks that keep a home operating and in training her children in their duties.

She is joyful, rejoicing in the blessings she bestows upon her household. She dispenses charity and hospitality.

Her mouth is full of wisdom. Her tongue reflects a gracious spirit.

Most of the discussion on submission has so far been devoted to the recognition of authority, largely because this is such an issue at the present time. Subjection to authority is only a part of the concept of submission.

FOR THE PROFIT
OF ANOTHER

The real essence of submission is demonstrated when one *voluntarily* gives one's self and one's ability to benefit another.

Practicing Christians ought to have no difficultv grasping the concept of submitting one's life to bring glory to another.

Note the model woman again. The emphasis is not placed on her subordination to her husband's authority. In fact this whole submission/authority thing operates best when it operates quietly and unobtrusively. The finest leadership operates without calling attention to itself. The noblest submission is without flattering lip service.

Indeed, rather than stressing her submission to authority, this woman is pictured as a person of influence herself.

Her husband was a smart man. He knew the dividends he would reap by investing authority in her. Furthermore, he safeguarded his investment by upholding her in the position she deserved as an intelligent capable woman.

Emphasis is placed on the goal to which she directs her efforts. Note the expressions:

"She will do him (her husband) good . . . all the days of her life."

"Her husband is known in the gates, when he sits among the leaders of the land."

She is principally motivated towards and rewarded by the increased prestige she brings to her husband and her household. Abilities that could have been used to make a name for herself, she re-directs to the credit of her husband.

Her husband is in the limelight, a light that would not be so bright were he shining alone. She knows this. So does everyone else. Her work of art is on display. This is her praise.

Does an artist feel demeaned because the light shines on her canvas and not on her?

REWARD

There is yet a third concept to submission that further distinguishes it from suppression. That is the concept of reward. Suppression is akin to slavery, a relationship in which one has no rightful claim to remuneration. This is not the case with one who offers to serve.

It is the obligation of the one receiving submission to recompense the one offering it.

Apply the latter two principles to labor relations. Every employee offers to work with the primary motive of enriching the employer. Every employer ensures the payment of fair and appropriate reward.

IN THE HOME

Note again with our model:

" . . . Her children rise up and call her blessed; her husband also and he praises her."

"Give her of the fruit of her hands: and let her own works praise her in the gates."

This woman is not found only in ancient Hebrew literature, she is to be found everywhere. In spite of the attempts by the female liberation front to discourage them from it, most women would, within the limitations of their individual ability, willingly provide the same service to their husbands today and feel fulfilled in so doing if their husbands would only allow them to try and then reward them with the love and praise they deserve.

The principle reward is not monetary, though a woman should share in the benefits of her husband's level of prosperity.

A faultless man will, of course, expect faultless service. A good man will credit willing service. He will reward intent rather than criticize failure.

In marriage, a man and a woman unite as two hands clasped, the fingers intertwined, as Bob Mumford so beautifully illustrates. It is not the case of one armored fist engulfing and crushing other.

With most people one hand is dominant. One hand wields the hammer. The other hand holds the nail. Stupid is the man who hammers his helping hand.

Chapter 8

HEALING THE WOUNDS THROUGH LOVE

"I can't love my husband anymore."

"How can you ask me to forgive my wife after all she has done? I can't forgive her."

"She has hurt me too often. I don't feel any love for her now. What is more, I would be a hypocrite if I tried to show her love."

"I should forgive *him!!!* You talk as if *I* was the guilty one — that *I* should make the move. I caught him red-handed this time. I can never forgive him."

These are the remarks of people who have been hurt. It is doubtful if any marriage proceeds without a measure of pain. Some marriages are very painful. Trouble is not the criterion for declaring a mismatch.

Some people are more gentle, softer by nature, more easily placated. They find it easier to adjust. Others are more easily hurt, more volatile and less flexible. For them molding is painful and is not accomplished without the stress of their circumstances and the intense heat of their own making.

WOUNDED NOT MUTILATED

The most sincere lovers will wound each other. In the initial stages, at least, the wounds are unintentional, but they hurt nevertheless. A wound does not make you an amputee. It is possible to be wounded and yet remain a whole person. You probably thought you would never recover that first serious breach, but you did. You thought you were crippled for life, but you were not.

Our usual response to hurt is anger and resentment. Having become accustomed to the feeling of love toward your adored, these very different emotions may come as a bit of a shock.

FACE FEELINGS FRANKLY

If they are not dealt with, they have a way of hanging around for days at a time, brooding and multiplying. Like bacteria, they thrive in the dark. Brought into the open, they lose much of their strength. How do you account for the presence of such feelings in a concord engineered in heaven?

These hurts and their attendant feelings may be the first unwelcome testimonial that your marriage is actually earthy and your idol, human, made of the same cheap clay as the rest of us.

Such wounds are to be anticipated. Cleansed with forgiveness and love they will heal without scar or disfigurement. Contaminated with resentment and self-pity they refuse to heal. Lying like smoldering volcanoes below the surface, buried hurts color the most innocent present events with the memory of past offenses and distort communications between husband and wife.

DEAL POSITIVELY WITH THE NEGATIVE

Many people have never learned to express negative feelings, indeed are afraid of them, feel guilty about them and try to bury them out of sight. Such feelings present a ticklish management problem. If we were given to more rigid self-discipline we might simply identify them, pronounce a judgment against them, then refuse them any influence over our behavior. It would appear that for many people, this line of approach has been distorted to judging the disaffection as reprehensible, then disguising it beyond recognition so it's existence can be more easily denied. There it remains hidden yet subconsciously influencing us to some unseeming behavior while we blissfully make great protestations of love.

Wrath, animosity, hatred, resentment, hostility and a host of fellow travellers are mean and injurious companions at best. They are not rendered any less malignant by pretending they are not present. Self-deception has no purifying qualities. Until one learns to respond in love to even unpleasant situations, it is of inestimable value to honestly acknowledge one's real feelings, however negative.

HATE DESTROYS THE HATER

Christ taught his disciples to deal with their enemies in love. Most of our conflicts are with people much closer to us than enemies. How much more should the difficulties in these relationships be handled in love?

Christ's purpose in his instruction is two-fold. It is his nature to love and he wants his disciples to participate in his nature. Furthermore, learning to act in love rather than reacting in hatred has self-protective qualities.

The poisonous effects of hatred and

bitterness have long been recognized. It remains for each one of us to realize that hatred's real victim is the one who is possessed by it. Hatred is a strange poison. It destroys the vessel in which it is stored.

HONESTY WITHOUT WISDOM

For some it comes as quite a shock to realize what feelings they have been carrying around.

The problem for other people is they feel that honesty demands that they act out their feelings. This really blows the lid off Pandora's box.

If they feel love for someone, honesty demands they must go to bed. If they feel hurt, they must act spitefully. To act contrary to their feelings would to them be considered hypocrisy.

Expressing one's feelings in terms of honestly and objectively declaring them, may well lead to repair. Expressing them in terms of obeying the impulse of one's feelings can be nothing less than destructive.

For instance A and B have had some rough times. The feeling of love is much less in evidence. The feelings of hurt, frustration and disappointment are much more a part of the scene. They demonstrate these feelings. The hurts are compounded. It would seem they are no longer in love. One day, much to his surprise, A begins to feel vibrations from C. He returns them. Wow! He is in love — again. His idea of honesty dictates he must leave B, whom he *no longer loves* (the love is gone; he no longer feels love; he can no longer love her) and move in with C whom he madly loves. You may label this honesty, but you would be several jumps ahead if you called it by its right name; confusion.

We always feel better when we can get God on our side, so run it through this way.

The basis of marriage is love (an uncertain premise).

God is love.

The love is all gone from this marriage (that is the feeling has not been around for awhile). Our relationship is no longer based on love.

This relationship is, therefore, not the will of God (a conclusion that gradually adapts itself to: it never was the will of God).

I'm in love with someone else (i.e. the feelings have been pretty strong lately).

God is love (an important recollection at this precise moment).

Therefore it must be God's will to dissolve the present (unloving) relationship and move in (temporarily at least) with the one I love.

The above exercise is not a progression of logic; it is regression through emotional and mental deception.

It may come as a surprise to many people, especially is it a surprise to happily married people, that they are still susceptible to third party vibrations. Given a bit of encouragement after the initial shock, such feelings can get quite exciting. If this situation arises during a period of marital discord, the person whose feelings are the master of his or her actions, is likely to make foolish decisions with chaotic consequences.

Honesty would allow you to acknowledge your feelings, at least to yourself. Wisdom would demand you nip your emotions in the bud. There is more to manhood and womanhood than the ability to seduce and be seduced.

We are all aware that love has feeling and I'm sure we all like the feeling. You have every right to want the feeling and every right to experience it. You have also the obligation to conduct your life on a level above the instability of feeling-centred decisions.

LOVE IS MORE
THAN FEELING

Love goes beyond doing what comes naturally. It is built of more solid stuff than a blush and a bag full of instinct. When we speak of romantic love, eroticism or passion or even the feeling component of parental, sibling and brotherly love we are talking about the icing on the cake. It is delightful, provided there is something of substance under it.

The enraptured young parents ogle their new-born in the early evening. Love is there. Love is felt. The same infant's midnight cry could go well unheeded, if feelings are the limit of his mother's love. Rising out of a warm bed to care for a wet and hungry infant may be quite contrary to her feelings at that hour.

To love is something that must be learned. The early church made it the responsibility of mature persons *to teach* young persons to love; to love their spouses; to love their children.[1] Love is an act; an act of kindness based on something more stable than feelings alone.

Who has not had the feeling of love depart, temporarily at least? For a period of time the only emotion experienced may be one of hurt, anger or frustration. At such a time love ceases to be a function of the emotion and becomes a function of the will.

The remarks quoted at the opening of this chapter are made by people who have suffered severe and often repetitive hurts. The statement "I can't love him or her any longer" is understandable but actually incorrect.

---

1. Titus 2:4

My usual response is "You are not really telling me the truth. It isn't that you can't love or that you can't forgive. It is that you won't. You won't forgive. You won't love."

Those who say they do not feel love and therefore cannot be expected to show love are in part the prisoners of their own wounded feelings and in part the victims of a pleasure and feeling-oriented philosophy, a philosophy in which one worships at the altar of pleasure and sacrifices everything to it, in which people are the servants and not the masters of their feelings.

The most widely acclaimed essay on love[1] does not describe a single emotion. It addresses itself to the intent toward and the treatment of another person.

The foundation of a marriage, the quality goods beneath the icing, is the imperfect but consistent acts and responses of love; kindness determined by another's need rather than one's own whims.

It is not hypocrisy to be very aware of hurt, frustration and anger and yet act in kindness and good will. It is not an act of hypocrisy to honestly tell your husband he has hurt you, to allow your voice to carry the emotional component of your pain, to let him realize your frustration and hurt and having done all this, still serve him a

1. I Corinthians: 13

111

delicious dinner: without strichnine. Under similar circumstances, the husband can act in a similar manner.

LOVE BY COMMITMENT

Brief mention has been made of the four concepts of love described by four Greek words. Of these Agape love must play the greatest part in the love of married people.

Erotic love is bound to the emotion and must wax and wane with one's mood. Agape love is the substance beneath it that brings stability and security.

This is love by decision, love by covenant, love by commitment, love as an exercise of the will. I won't try to second guess what was in your mind when you pledged yourself ... I will love ... but, giving some thought to it now, you must realize you were not saying "I will feel love," "my love will depend on the fluctuation of my feeling." No. You were making a commitment of your will.

"I will love you" becomes akin to "I will to love you." I love you because I *will* to love you. I've made a choice. I've made a decision. I'm committing myself to live by that decision.

Love desires the best for another. It reaches out in continuing good will even toward the one who has brought offense.

It is not a matter of waiting for the right feeling before you do the right thing. It is a matter of doing the right thing, and invariably the feeling will begin to accompany it.

In our society we enter marriage after falling in love. For millions of people marriage is arranged by parents. The bride and groom remain total strangers until the wedding. There is no reason to believe that falling in love is an all-important forerunner to a sound marriage. I am not suggesting that people raised in our culture should marry without experiencing the feeling of love. I simply wish to make the point that the mature decisions to treat another person lovingly, and to put his or her needs ahead of your own, is as much the evidence of love as all the passion of the great lovers enshrined in classical literature.

This is not a put-down on emotion, but marriage is a game for mature players only. The maturity to make solid commitment, to act lovingly, will enhance your part in the passion play.

You have been wounded. Your partner has bled a bit as well. Sometimes you have been absolutely baffled to see an act of good intention produce a response of pain. At other times you have drawn blood out of revenge. You have both withdrawn to a safe distance apart and built up elaborate defenses. You have learned to be suspicious and resentful. You can also learn to be loving.

Your only hope to see the wall removed

is the re-establishment of trust based on consistent, sincere good will demonstrated in word and in deed. Initially, the decision to stop acting spitefully and to start acting lovingly may have to be unilateral. Don't wait for your partner to make the first move. Start today.

To be loved is everyone's birthright. To love is everyone's obligation.

Chapter 9

HEALING THE WOUNDS THROUGH FORGIVENESS

Some time ago a popular song sounded out the message that to love is to never say I'm sorry. Following that trend of thought, the frequency with which we must say "I'm sorry" is an indication of how often we are unthoughtful and unloving.

Our thoughtless misdemeanors, or downright malicious deeds, produce in us a sense of guilt. Guilt is painful. We may mask the feeling to spare ourselves the pain. When we wrong another we stand morally guilty whether we feel it or not.

The only cure for guilt is forgiveness, forgiveness from the one against whom we committed the offense.

Sometimes our pride keeps us from saying "I'm sorry." Just as often our pride keeps us from saying "I forgive you."

Forgiveness is not a matter of can or

can't. It is a matter of will or won't. When you don't forgive, it is because you won't.

Forgiveness does not depend on an apology. The statement, "I can't forgive him because he has never said he was sorry," expresses a misconception.

Forgiveness can be a unilateral act following on a unilateral decision. Smoldering resentment is a game easily adapted to solitary play. Well nursed, your wrath can be held at boiling point for years. Since the fire is burning in you, it requires only you to put it out.

A disciple asked Jesus how often one should forgive an offender; seven times? The reply was if someone offended you, tell him (let him know clamly, objectively, if possible, but at any rate let him know) that he has been hitting below the belt. If he repents, forgive him, not seven times but seventy times seven.[1]

What happens if the offender doesn't repent? You forgive anyway. Christ further taught that forgiveness does not depend upon the repentance of the offender. He taught that if anyone offends, you are to forgive the offender the next time you came to pray.[2]

It seems that an unforgiving attitude impedes communication with God. It also

---

1. Mathew 18: 21,22
2. Mark 11: 25,26

wreaks havoc with communication between people.

THE ROOT OF BITTERNESS

One of the hazards of divorce and re-marriage is the failure to forgive the offenses of the former partner. As you sit grimly grinding your hatchet, reminding yourself of the treachery of your ex-spouse, you are supersensitive to any indication that your present spouse might repeat the performance of the former. A past, unhappy and unforgiven experience with one person leads you to conclude "they are all the same."

You don't have to do a thing to have weeds ruin your garden. Just leave them there. You don't have to do a thing to have bitterness spoil personal relationships. Just allow the root to remain, it will bear fruit without further effort on your part. The emotional charge attached to a past, unforgiven event will continue to cloud your communication long after the offense has ceased.

Like love, forgiveness is dependent upon our will.

There is no good reason for the lack of forgiveness apart from the refusal to forgive.

Forgiveness does not depend on the cessation of offenses. While they were in the process of crucifying him, Jesus said, "Father, forgive them." One hopes the offense would cease, particularly that it should not continue repetitiously. Yet in the face of continuing offense, one can determine not to build up the barriers, but to keep open the avenues of communication to allow the flow of love, peace and good will.

Forgiveness does not depend on receiving compensation. It is reasonable, when possible, that recompense should be made for the offense. This may not be possible. Often all one can do is say, "I'm sorry. Please forgive me."

Forgiveness does not exactly imply forgetting. In fact some people are better at forgetting than they are at forgiving. They still carry a grudge long after a clear recall of the details has escaped them.

Not that that really matters. I've always found that if you have enough resentment, your imagination can always manufacture details to suit the occasion.

Rather than implying that you drop from your intellect the memory of the event, forgiveness means you drop or remove the emotional response to that event. The incidental recall of the facts no longer makes the kettle boil.

You defuse the bomb. You may remember, but you don't repeat at future altercations the sordid details of the forgiven offense. You remove the emotional charge formerly associated with the event. These emotions cease to have an influence on your response to the person you have forgiven.

Historically, the event is a fact. Emotionally, it never happened.

You remove the barriers between yourself and the offender, barriers you erected at the time of the offense and once again open the channel of communication to allow the flow of love, joy and good will.

COURAGE

Forgiveness requires courage. When you take the offending person back into your life, you set yourself up to the risk of being hurt again. She might do it again.

In fact, you expose yourself to the peril of injury when you open your life to anyone. That is the risk you take in any close personal relationship. You cannot avoid the risk and have the relationship.

We all thought when we entered marriage that matrimony would bring out the best in us. Instead it brought out *everything* in us, the best *and the worst*. While we are smarting from the hurts, we fix our attention so completely on the faults that our partner's finer qualities become obscured.

RESENTMENT PROVIDES
AN EXCUSE

There are reasons why people refuse to forgive. There is an interesting story told of the visit of Jesus to a place that sheltered people who came in hope of a miracle of healing. He talked to a man who had been there forty years. He asked him, "Do you want to be made whole?"

That seems like a ridiculous question at first hearing — asking a man if he wants what he has spent forty years trying to get. It is not at all senseless though.

In effect the question is this, "Do you know that if you are healed you can no longer lie here and depend on other people's charity. If you are made whole, you will have to return to your community and contribute to it and to your family as a whole man. You will no longer have a reason to be excused from your responsibilities."

As a result of the battle wounds, you have withdrawn from full-time participation in your marriage. Your resentment is a source of protection and an excuse, an excuse to be less than a normal person. You can say,

"How can he expect me to respond to him as a whole person after what he has done to me? I'm wounded, and he did it. He can't expect me to be the same as I was before he abused me."

"How can she expect me to be a decent husband to her after the way she has treated me."

A CRUTCH

Your hostility and resentment, the grudge you carry, are a continuing evidence that you have been crippled. No one has the right to expect as much from a crippled person. You can lean on your handicap. The bruises on your skin disappeared with time. Now if you allow forgiveness to lance the boil in your emotions and drain away the purulence of self-pity you will be without evidence of your injury. You will have no excuse to withhold part or all of your expected contribution. People will live for years under this emotional strain, their stomachs ulcerated, their blood pressure elevated, their heads aching, their marriage stalemated while they nurse a twenty year old grievance, clinging to it as an excuse for being less than a whole person.

A REFUGE

Even after a separation, people will hold onto their resentment, fearing that if they forgive, they will be expected to return to the former unwholesome situation. Their grudge is their protective hiding place. That must be the most costly protection racket going.

AN AXE

Your resentment is a weapon you can hold over your partner's head. If anyone ever praises him or if he tries to raise his head above his heels, you can flash his offenses before him and show him (and the whole world if you choose) what a dirty rotter he really is.

She has hurt you, but now you have the means of getting your pound of flesh in return. If you forgive, you will lose this advantage and miss your opportunity for revenge. If you forgive, you will have to bury the hatchet somewhere other than between her shoulder blades. You don't want to forgive. Revenge is too sweet.

In one of my travels, I counselled the widow of a prominent physician. She complained of depression. Initially, I thought it was a bereavement but it became obvious her depression was related to the memories of his mistreatment of her, actions that probably would have shocked his closest friends. After awhile I suggested she forgive him.

She said typically, "I can't."

"You are not telling me the truth. The truth is you won't."

"You won't because if you do you will have to lay down the axe. You have a powerful weapon. You can reach even beyond his grave to mar his public image anytime you choose. You could let people, his relatives, his patients, anyone, know what he was really like at home. If you forgive him, you won't be able to do that. Even now, having kept it all to yourself, you can sit in smug self-righteousness that even though you could do so you are too noble to hurt him as he hurt you. You will also lose that if you forgive him."

She forgave him, posthumously. Her depression lifted. No one may ever know what a mean rascal he was, but she is as happy as a clam at high tide. To grant forgiveness is even sweeter than to gain vengence.

"God, from my heart I forgive everyone for everything they ever did against me."

Healing a marriage requires sincere determination, the maturity to consider the needs and security of your partner as more important than your own, the honesty to openly cleanse the wounds, and the courage to pour in love and forgiveness.

BOUND BY BRUISES

Some people have been so badly wounded, that they really are not untruthful when they say they cannot love, they cannot forgive. They are so bruised they are unable to act as whole persons.

We have to reach beyond ourselves and find the power to change our natural responses, to repay evil with good, to love those who spitefully abuse us. That is the secret of rehabilitation.

I believe in God. Christ said he was empowered of the Spirit of God to set at liberty bruised men and women.[1] Ask Him to give you the power to forgive those who have injured you.

---

1. Luke 4:18